50 French Kiss Cookbook Recipes

By: Kelly Johnson

Table of Contents

- Croissant Benedict
- Ratatouille Tart
- Parisian Crêpes Suzette
- Duck Confit Salad
- Lobster Bisque au Vin Blanc
- Coq au Vin
- Pâté en Croûte
- French Onion Soup Gratinée
- Bouillabaisse Provencale
- Truffle Fries with Aioli
- Steak Frites au Poivre
- Escargots de Bourgogne
- Quiche Lorraine
- Croque Monsieur
- Chocolate Soufflé
- Tarte Tatin
- Lemon Madeleines

- Salade Niçoise
- Beef Wellington à la Française
- Brie and Fig Jam Crostini
- Tarte au Citron
- Cassoulet de Toulouse
- Pissaladière Provençale
- Sole Meunière
- Bouche de Noël
- Chateaubriand with Béarnaise
- Gratin Dauphinois
- Duck à l'Orange
- French Toast with Crème Brûlée Sauce
- Vichyssoise
- Mille-feuille
- Roquefort and Pear Salad
- Clafoutis aux Cerises
- Moules Marinières
- Fennel and Orange Salad
- Poulet Rôti with Herbes de Provence

- Crème Caramel
- Gâteau de Crêpes
- Filet Mignon au Jus
- Caramelized Onion and Goat Cheese Tart
- Chèvre with Honey and Walnuts
- Tartare de Bœuf
- Madeleines au Chocolat
- Salmon en Papillote
- Pan-seared Foie Gras with Balsamic Reduction
- Mousse au Chocolat
- French Pistachio Macarons
- Canelés de Bordeaux
- Pâtisserie du Jour
- Pistachio Frangipane Tart

Croissant Benedict
Ingredients

- 2 croissants, split
- 4 eggs
- 1/2 cup hollandaise sauce (store-bought or homemade)
- 4 slices Canadian bacon
- Fresh chives for garnish

Instructions

1. Toast the croissants until golden brown.
2. Poach the eggs to your desired doneness.
3. Warm the Canadian bacon slices in a pan.
4. Assemble by layering the toasted croissant halves with Canadian bacon and poached eggs.
5. Pour hollandaise sauce over the top and garnish with fresh chives.

Ratatouille Tart

Ingredients

- 1 sheet puff pastry
- 1 zucchini, thinly sliced
- 1 eggplant, thinly sliced
- 1 red bell pepper, thinly sliced
- 1 yellow squash, thinly sliced
- 2 tbsp olive oil
- 1 tsp dried thyme
- 1/2 tsp garlic powder
- Salt and pepper to taste
- Fresh basil for garnish

Instructions

1. Preheat oven to 375°F (190°C).
2. Roll out puff pastry onto a baking sheet and prick the base with a fork.
3. Arrange zucchini, eggplant, bell pepper, and squash in a spiral pattern over the pastry.
4. Drizzle with olive oil, sprinkle with thyme, garlic powder, salt, and pepper.
5. Bake for 25-30 minutes until pastry is golden and vegetables are tender.
6. Garnish with fresh basil before serving.

Parisian Crêpes Suzette

Ingredients

- 4 crêpes (either store-bought or homemade)
- 1/4 cup orange juice
- 1/4 cup Grand Marnier
- 1 tbsp orange zest
- 1/4 cup butter
- 2 tbsp sugar
- 2 tbsp lemon juice

Instructions

1. Make or heat crêpes and set them aside.
2. In a pan, melt butter and sugar together until bubbly.
3. Add orange juice, zest, and lemon juice, stirring to combine.
4. Fold the crêpes into quarters and place them in the pan with the sauce.
5. Add Grand Marnier, flame the crêpes (optional), and cook until the sauce thickens.
6. Serve the crêpes with the sauce drizzled over them.

Duck Confit Salad

Ingredients

- 2 duck legs confit, shredded
- 4 cups mixed greens (arugula, spinach, etc.)
- 1/2 cup sliced roasted beets
- 1/4 cup goat cheese, crumbled
- 1/4 cup toasted walnuts
- 1/4 cup balsamic vinaigrette

Instructions

1. Shred the duck confit and set aside.
2. In a large bowl, combine mixed greens, roasted beets, goat cheese, and walnuts.
3. Add the shredded duck confit on top.
4. Drizzle with balsamic vinaigrette and toss gently to combine.

Lobster Bisque au Vin Blanc

Ingredients

- 1 lb lobster meat, cooked and chopped
- 4 cups seafood stock
- 1/2 cup dry white wine (vin blanc)
- 1/2 cup heavy cream
- 1 onion, finely chopped
- 2 garlic cloves, minced
- 1 tbsp tomato paste
- 2 tbsp butter
- 1/4 tsp cayenne pepper
- Salt and pepper to taste

Instructions

1. In a pot, melt butter and sauté onion and garlic until soft.
2. Stir in tomato paste, cayenne pepper, and white wine.
3. Add seafood stock and bring to a simmer.
4. Pour in the heavy cream and add the lobster meat, cooking until the soup is heated through.
5. Season with salt and pepper, then blend the soup for a smooth texture.
6. Serve with a drizzle of cream and extra lobster pieces.

Coq au Vin

Ingredients

- 4 chicken thighs, bone-in
- 1 cup red wine (Burgundy is traditional)
- 1/2 cup chicken broth
- 2 tbsp olive oil
- 1 onion, chopped
- 3 garlic cloves, minced
- 2 carrots, sliced
- 1/2 cup pearl onions, peeled
- 1 cup mushrooms, sliced
- 2 tbsp tomato paste
- 2 bay leaves
- 1 tsp thyme
- Salt and pepper to taste

Instructions

1. In a large pot, brown chicken thighs in olive oil, then set aside.
2. In the same pot, sauté onion, garlic, carrots, and mushrooms until softened.
3. Stir in tomato paste, wine, chicken broth, and herbs.

4. Return chicken to the pot, cover, and simmer for 45 minutes until chicken is tender.

5. Serve with mashed potatoes or crusty bread.

Pâté en Croûte

Ingredients

- 1 lb ground pork
- 1/2 lb ground veal
- 1/2 lb chicken liver, cleaned
- 1/4 cup brandy
- 1/4 tsp thyme
- 1/4 tsp sage
- 1 tbsp Dijon mustard
- 1 sheet puff pastry
- Salt and pepper to taste

Instructions

1. Mix the meats, livers, brandy, thyme, sage, mustard, salt, and pepper.
2. Roll out puff pastry and line a loaf pan.
3. Fill with the meat mixture and seal the pastry over the top.
4. Bake at 375°F (190°C) for 45 minutes until golden.
5. Let cool before slicing.

French Onion Soup Gratinée

Ingredients

- 4 large onions, sliced
- 4 cups beef broth
- 1/2 cup dry white wine
- 2 tbsp butter
- 2 tbsp olive oil
- 1 tsp thyme
- 2 bay leaves
- 1/2 baguette, sliced
- 1 cup Gruyère cheese, grated

Instructions

1. Caramelize onions in butter and olive oil over medium heat for 30 minutes.
2. Add white wine, thyme, bay leaves, and beef broth, simmering for 20 minutes.
3. Toast the baguette slices.
4. Ladle soup into bowls, top with a toasted slice of bread, and sprinkle with Gruyère cheese.
5. Broil until cheese is golden and bubbly.

Bouillabaisse Provencale

Ingredients

- 1 lb mixed seafood (fish, shrimp, mussels, etc.)
- 4 cups seafood stock
- 1 cup dry white wine
- 2 tomatoes, chopped
- 1 onion, sliced
- 2 garlic cloves, minced
- 1 fennel bulb, sliced
- 1 tbsp olive oil
- 1 tsp saffron threads
- 1 tsp orange zest
- 1/2 tsp thyme
- Salt and pepper to taste

Instructions

1. Sauté onion, garlic, fennel, and tomatoes in olive oil until soft.
2. Add seafood stock, white wine, saffron, orange zest, thyme, salt, and pepper.
3. Bring to a boil, then add the seafood.
4. Simmer for 15 minutes until seafood is cooked through.
5. Serve with a side of rouille and crusty bread.

Truffle Fries with Aioli

Ingredients

- 4 medium russet potatoes, cut into fries
- 2 tbsp olive oil
- 1 tbsp truffle oil
- 1/4 cup grated Parmesan cheese
- Salt to taste
- Fresh parsley for garnish

Aioli

- 1/2 cup mayonnaise
- 1 garlic clove, minced
- 1 tbsp lemon juice
- 1 tsp truffle oil
- Salt and pepper to taste

Instructions

1. Preheat oven to 400°F (200°C). Toss fries with olive oil, truffle oil, and salt.
2. Bake for 25-30 minutes until crispy.
3. For aioli, mix mayonnaise, garlic, lemon juice, truffle oil, salt, and pepper.
4. Serve fries with a side of aioli for dipping, garnished with Parmesan and parsley.

Steak Frites au Poivre

Ingredients

- 2 steaks (ribeye, filet mignon, or strip)
- 2 tbsp black peppercorns, crushed
- 2 tbsp butter
- 2 tbsp olive oil
- 1/2 cup brandy
- 1/2 cup heavy cream
- 1/2 cup beef stock
- Salt to taste
- Fresh parsley for garnish

Instructions

1. Season the steaks generously with crushed black pepper and salt.
2. In a pan, heat olive oil over medium-high heat. Sear the steaks for 4-5 minutes on each side for medium-rare, or to your preferred doneness.
3. Remove steaks from the pan and set aside. In the same pan, add butter and sauté the peppercorns for 1-2 minutes.
4. Add brandy and let it reduce by half. Stir in the beef stock and heavy cream, and simmer until the sauce thickens.
5. Serve the steaks with the pepper sauce drizzled over and garnish with fresh parsley. Serve with crispy fries.

Escargots de Bourgogne

Ingredients

- 24 escargots (snails), shelled
- 1/2 cup unsalted butter, softened
- 4 garlic cloves, minced
- 2 tbsp fresh parsley, chopped
- 1 tbsp fresh thyme leaves
- 1 tbsp shallots, finely chopped
- 1/4 cup dry white wine
- Salt and pepper to taste

Instructions

1. Preheat oven to 400°F (200°C).
2. In a bowl, mix softened butter with garlic, parsley, thyme, shallots, salt, and pepper.
3. Place escargots in escargot dishes or a baking pan and top each one with a dollop of the herb butter mixture.
4. Drizzle the wine around the escargots and bake for 10-15 minutes, or until the butter is bubbling and the snails are cooked through.
5. Serve with crusty bread to soak up the delicious sauce.

Quiche Lorraine

Ingredients

- 1 pie crust (store-bought or homemade)
- 6 large eggs
- 1 cup heavy cream
- 1 cup whole milk
- 1/2 lb bacon, chopped and cooked
- 1/2 cup Gruyère cheese, grated
- 1/4 cup Parmesan cheese, grated
- Salt and pepper to taste
- 1/4 tsp nutmeg

Instructions

1. Preheat oven to 375°F (190°C).
2. In a bowl, whisk together eggs, heavy cream, milk, nutmeg, salt, and pepper.
3. Spread cooked bacon evenly across the bottom of the pie crust, then sprinkle with Gruyère and Parmesan.
4. Pour the egg mixture over the bacon and cheese.
5. Bake for 35-40 minutes, or until the center is set and the top is lightly golden. Let cool slightly before slicing.

Croque Monsieur

Ingredients

- 8 slices French bread
- 4 slices ham
- 1 cup Gruyère cheese, grated
- 1 tbsp Dijon mustard
- 1/2 cup béchamel sauce (butter, flour, milk, salt, and nutmeg)
- 2 tbsp butter

Instructions

1. Preheat oven to 375°F (190°C).
2. Spread Dijon mustard on 4 slices of bread. Layer with ham and grated Gruyère cheese. Top with the remaining slices of bread.
3. Spread béchamel sauce on top of each sandwich, then sprinkle with more cheese.
4. Butter a baking dish and place the sandwiches inside. Bake for 15-20 minutes, until the cheese is melted and golden brown.

Chocolate Soufflé

Ingredients

- 4 oz dark chocolate
- 3 tbsp butter
- 3 large eggs, separated
- 1/4 cup sugar
- 1/4 tsp vanilla extract
- Pinch of salt
- Powdered sugar for dusting

Instructions

1. Preheat oven to 375°F (190°C) and butter 4 ramekins.
2. Melt chocolate and butter in a double boiler. Once melted, set aside to cool slightly.
3. Whisk egg yolks with sugar and vanilla until pale. Stir in the melted chocolate.
4. Beat egg whites with a pinch of salt until stiff peaks form.
5. Gently fold the egg whites into the chocolate mixture until just combined.
6. Spoon into ramekins and bake for 12-15 minutes, or until puffed and set. Dust with powdered sugar before serving.

Tarte Tatin

Ingredients

- 6-8 apples, peeled and cored
- 1/2 cup unsalted butter
- 1/2 cup sugar
- 1 tsp vanilla extract
- 1 sheet puff pastry
- 1 tbsp lemon juice

Instructions

1. Preheat oven to 375°F (190°C).
2. In a skillet, melt butter and sugar over medium heat until caramelized. Add apples, cut side down, and cook for 10-15 minutes until softened.
3. Remove from heat and drizzle with lemon juice.
4. Cover the apples with puff pastry and tuck the edges inside the skillet.
5. Bake for 25-30 minutes, until the pastry is golden and puffed.
6. Let cool slightly before inverting onto a plate and serving.

Lemon Madeleines

Ingredients

- 2 large eggs
- 1/2 cup sugar
- 1/2 tsp vanilla extract
- 1 tbsp lemon zest
- 1/2 cup flour
- 1/4 tsp baking powder
- 1/4 tsp salt
- 1/2 cup unsalted butter, melted
- Powdered sugar for dusting

Instructions

1. Preheat oven to 375°F (190°C) and grease madeleine pans.
2. Whisk eggs and sugar until light and fluffy. Stir in vanilla and lemon zest.
3. Sift flour, baking powder, and salt together and fold into the egg mixture.
4. Gradually add melted butter, mixing until combined.
5. Spoon batter into madeleine pans and bake for 10-12 minutes, until golden.
6. Dust with powdered sugar before serving.

Salade Niçoise

Ingredients

- 2 cups mixed greens
- 2 boiled eggs, quartered
- 1/2 lb tuna (fresh or canned in olive oil)
- 1/2 cup cherry tomatoes, halved
- 1/4 cup Kalamata olives
- 1/2 red onion, thinly sliced
- 1/2 cup green beans, blanched
- 1/4 cup olive oil
- 2 tbsp red wine vinegar
- 1 tsp Dijon mustard
- Salt and pepper to taste

Instructions

1. Arrange mixed greens on a platter. Top with tuna, eggs, tomatoes, olives, red onion, and green beans.
2. In a small bowl, whisk together olive oil, vinegar, mustard, salt, and pepper.
3. Drizzle dressing over the salad and serve.

Beef Wellington à la Française

Ingredients

- 1 lb beef tenderloin, trimmed
- 2 tbsp Dijon mustard
- 1/2 lb mushrooms, finely chopped
- 2 tbsp butter
- 1/4 cup pâté de foie gras (optional)
- 1 sheet puff pastry
- 1 egg, beaten
- Salt and pepper to taste

Instructions

1. Sear beef tenderloin in a hot pan with butter until browned on all sides. Let cool and brush with Dijon mustard.
2. Sauté chopped mushrooms until all moisture evaporates, then cool.
3. Spread pâté (if using) over the beef, then top with the mushroom mixture.
4. Wrap the beef in puff pastry, seal, and brush with beaten egg.
5. Bake at 400°F (200°C) for 30-40 minutes, or until golden and cooked to your liking.

Brie and Fig Jam Crostini

Ingredients

- 1 baguette, sliced
- 8 oz Brie cheese, sliced
- 1/4 cup fig jam
- Fresh thyme for garnish

Instructions

1. Preheat oven to 375°F (190°C).
2. Toast baguette slices in the oven for 5-7 minutes, until crisp.
3. Spread fig jam on each crostini and top with a slice of Brie.
4. Bake for an additional 5 minutes, until the cheese melts.
5. Garnish with fresh thyme and serve warm.

Tarte au Citron

Ingredients

- 1 pie crust (store-bought or homemade)
- 1 cup lemon juice
- 1 tbsp lemon zest
- 1 cup sugar
- 3 large eggs
- 1/2 cup heavy cream
- 1 tbsp butter, softened

Instructions

1. Preheat oven to 350°F (175°C).
2. In a bowl, whisk together lemon juice, zest, sugar, eggs, and cream.
3. Pour the filling into the pre-baked pie crust and bake for 25-30 minutes, until set.
4. Let cool completely before serving, dusted with powdered sugar.

Cassoulet de Toulouse

Ingredients

- 1 lb pork shoulder, cut into chunks
- 1 lb Toulouse sausage
- 1 lb duck confit, shredded
- 1 lb dried white beans (such as cannellini), soaked overnight
- 2 onions, chopped
- 4 garlic cloves, minced
- 2 carrots, chopped
- 2 celery stalks, chopped
- 1 cup chicken stock
- 1 tbsp tomato paste
- 1 tsp thyme
- 1 bay leaf
- Salt and pepper to taste
- 2 tbsp olive oil

Instructions

1. In a large pot, heat olive oil over medium heat and brown the pork and sausage. Set aside.

2. In the same pot, sauté onions, carrots, celery, and garlic until softened. Add tomato paste and cook for 1 minute.

3. Add the soaked beans, stock, thyme, and bay leaf. Bring to a simmer and cook for 1 hour, until beans are tender.

4. Add the browned pork, sausage, and shredded duck confit to the pot. Simmer for an additional 1-2 hours, until flavors meld and the beans are very soft.

5. Season with salt and pepper to taste before serving.

Pissaladière Provençale
Ingredients

- 1 pizza dough or pâte brisée (shortcrust pastry)
- 2 large onions, thinly sliced
- 2 tbsp olive oil
- 2 cloves garlic, minced
- 1 cup black olives, pitted
- 4 anchovy fillets
- 1 tsp thyme
- Salt and pepper to taste

Instructions

1. Preheat oven to 400°F (200°C).

2. In a large pan, heat olive oil and sauté the onions and garlic over low heat until they are very soft and caramelized, about 25 minutes.

3. Roll out the pizza dough or pastry and place it on a baking sheet.

4. Spread the caramelized onions evenly over the dough, then top with olives, anchovies, and thyme.

5. Bake for 20-25 minutes, until golden and crisp. Slice and serve warm.

Sole Meunière
Ingredients

- 2 sole fillets
- 1/4 cup flour
- 4 tbsp butter
- 2 tbsp lemon juice
- 2 tbsp parsley, chopped
- Salt and pepper to taste

Instructions

1. Dredge the sole fillets in flour, shaking off any excess.

2. Heat 2 tbsp butter in a large skillet over medium-high heat. Cook the fillets for 2-3 minutes on each side, until golden brown.

3. Remove the fish and set aside. In the same skillet, melt the remaining butter and add lemon juice.

4. Pour the butter sauce over the fish and sprinkle with parsley. Serve immediately.

Bouche de Noël
Ingredients

- 1 sponge cake (yule log)
- 1 1/2 cups heavy cream
- 2 tbsp powdered sugar
- 1 tsp vanilla extract
- 2 tbsp cocoa powder
- 1/2 cup chocolate ganache (melted chocolate and cream)

Instructions

1. Roll the sponge cake into a log and set aside.
2. Whip the cream with powdered sugar and vanilla until soft peaks form.
3. Unroll the cake and spread a layer of whipped cream inside. Re-roll the cake and cover the entire log with the remaining cream.
4. Dust the top with cocoa powder and drizzle with chocolate ganache to create a bark effect.
5. Chill before serving, garnished with edible holly leaves if desired.

Chateaubriand with Béarnaise
Ingredients

- 1 lb beef tenderloin, center cut
- 2 tbsp olive oil
- 2 tbsp butter
- Salt and pepper to taste

For Béarnaise Sauce:

- 1/2 cup white wine vinegar
- 1/2 cup white wine
- 1 small shallot, minced
- 1 tbsp tarragon, chopped
- 4 egg yolks
- 1 cup butter, melted
- Salt and pepper to taste

Instructions

1. Preheat oven to 400°F (200°C).
2. Heat olive oil and butter in a skillet over medium-high heat. Season the beef with salt and pepper and sear on all sides until browned.
3. Transfer to the oven and roast for 15-20 minutes for medium-rare. Let rest for 5 minutes before slicing.

4. To make the Béarnaise sauce, combine vinegar, wine, shallot, and tarragon in a saucepan and simmer until reduced by half.

5. Whisk egg yolks in a bowl and slowly add the reduction, then whisk in melted butter until the sauce thickens. Season with salt and pepper.

6. Serve the Chateaubriand with Béarnaise sauce drizzled over the top.

Gratin Dauphinois

Ingredients

- 2 lbs potatoes, thinly sliced
- 1 1/2 cups heavy cream
- 1/2 cup milk
- 2 garlic cloves, minced
- 2 tbsp butter
- 1 cup Gruyère cheese, grated
- Salt and pepper to taste

Instructions

1. Preheat oven to 375°F (190°C).
2. In a saucepan, heat the cream, milk, garlic, butter, salt, and pepper until just simmering.
3. In a buttered baking dish, layer the potato slices, pouring a bit of the cream mixture over each layer.
4. Top with grated cheese and bake for 45-60 minutes, until golden brown and bubbly. Let cool slightly before serving.

Duck à l'Orange

Ingredients

- 2 duck breasts
- 1/2 cup orange juice
- 1/4 cup chicken stock
- 1 tbsp sugar
- 1 tbsp vinegar
- 1/2 tsp orange zest
- 2 tbsp butter
- Salt and pepper to taste

Instructions

1. Season the duck breasts with salt and pepper and sear in a hot pan, skin side down, for 6-8 minutes until the skin is crispy. Flip and cook for another 4-5 minutes. Remove and let rest.

2. In the same pan, add sugar and vinegar and cook until caramelized. Add orange juice, chicken stock, and orange zest, stirring to combine.

3. Simmer the sauce for 5 minutes until it thickens.

4. Whisk in butter and pour over the duck before serving.

French Toast with Crème Brûlée Sauce

Ingredients

- 4 slices of brioche or thick-cut bread
- 2 eggs
- 1/2 cup milk
- 1 tbsp vanilla extract
- 1 tbsp butter
- 2 tbsp sugar
- 1/4 cup heavy cream

Instructions

1. Whisk together eggs, milk, vanilla, and sugar.
2. Dip the bread slices into the egg mixture, ensuring they're fully coated.
3. In a skillet, melt butter over medium heat and cook the French toast for 2-3 minutes on each side, until golden brown.
4. To make the crème brûlée sauce, heat cream in a saucepan. Whisk the sugar and egg yolks together until smooth, then pour in the hot cream slowly while whisking.
5. Serve the French toast with the crème brûlée sauce drizzled on top.

Vichyssoise

Ingredients

- 4 leeks, cleaned and chopped
- 2 large potatoes, peeled and diced
- 4 cups chicken stock
- 1/2 cup heavy cream
- 2 tbsp butter
- Salt and pepper to taste
- Chives for garnish

Instructions

1. Melt butter in a pot and sauté leeks until softened. Add potatoes and chicken stock, bring to a boil, then simmer for 20 minutes.
2. Puree the soup with an immersion blender or in a blender until smooth.
3. Stir in heavy cream, season with salt and pepper, and chill for at least 2 hours.
4. Garnish with chives before serving.

Mille-feuille

Ingredients

- 1 sheet puff pastry
- 1 cup pastry cream
- Powdered sugar for dusting

Instructions

1. Preheat oven to 400°F (200°C).
2. Roll out puff pastry and cut into 3 equal strips. Bake according to package instructions until golden and puffed.
3. Once cool, layer the puff pastry with pastry cream. Repeat for 2 more layers.
4. Dust the top with powdered sugar and serve immediately.

Roquefort and Pear Salad

Ingredients

- Mixed greens (arugula, frisée, baby spinach)
- 2 ripe pears, thinly sliced
- 1/3 cup crumbled Roquefort cheese
- 1/4 cup toasted walnuts
- 2 tbsp honey
- 1 tbsp balsamic vinegar
- 3 tbsp extra virgin olive oil
- Salt and pepper to taste

Instructions

1. Whisk together olive oil, balsamic vinegar, honey, salt, and pepper for the dressing.
2. Toss greens with pears, walnuts, and Roquefort.
3. Drizzle with dressing just before serving.

Clafoutis aux Cerises (Cherry Clafoutis)

Ingredients

- 2 cups fresh cherries, pitted
- 3 eggs
- 1/2 cup sugar
- 1 cup milk
- 1/2 cup all-purpose flour
- 1 tsp vanilla extract
- Pinch of salt
- Powdered sugar for dusting

Instructions

1. Preheat oven to 350°F (175°C).
2. Butter a baking dish and scatter cherries evenly.
3. Whisk eggs, sugar, vanilla, and salt. Add flour and then milk gradually to form a smooth batter.
4. Pour over cherries and bake 35–40 minutes until puffed and golden.
5. Let cool slightly and dust with powdered sugar.

Moules Marinières (Sailor-Style Mussels)

Ingredients

- 2 lbs fresh mussels, cleaned
- 1 cup dry white wine
- 2 shallots, minced
- 2 garlic cloves, minced
- 2 tbsp butter
- 1/2 cup heavy cream (optional)
- 1 tbsp chopped parsley
- Salt and pepper to taste

Instructions

1. In a large pot, melt butter and sauté shallots and garlic.
2. Add wine, bring to a boil, then add mussels. Cover and cook until they open (5–7 minutes).
3. Discard unopened mussels. Stir in cream (if using), season, and top with parsley.

Fennel and Orange Salad

Ingredients

- 2 fennel bulbs, thinly sliced
- 2 oranges, segmented
- 1/4 red onion, thinly sliced
- 2 tbsp olive oil
- 1 tbsp lemon juice
- Salt and pepper to taste

Instructions

1. Whisk lemon juice and olive oil together for a light dressing.
2. Toss fennel, oranges, and red onion in the dressing.
3. Chill and serve fresh.

Poulet Rôti with Herbes de Provence

Ingredients

- 1 whole chicken (3–4 lbs)
- 2 tbsp Herbes de Provence
- 3 tbsp olive oil
- Salt and pepper to taste
- 1 lemon, halved
- 4 garlic cloves

Instructions

1. Preheat oven to 425°F (220°C).
2. Rub the chicken with olive oil, Herbes de Provence, salt, and pepper. Stuff with lemon and garlic.
3. Roast for 1 to 1.5 hours, basting occasionally, until juices run clear. Let rest 10 minutes before carving.

Crème Caramel

Ingredients

- 1 cup sugar (for caramel)
- 1/4 cup water
- 2 cups whole milk
- 4 eggs
- 1 tsp vanilla extract
- 1/2 cup sugar (for custard)

Instructions

1. Melt 1 cup sugar with water until golden. Pour into ramekins to set as caramel.
2. Heat milk. Whisk eggs, 1/2 cup sugar, and vanilla, then temper with warm milk.
3. Pour custard over caramel.
4. Bake in a water bath at 325°F (160°C) for 40 minutes. Chill, then invert to serve.

Gâteau de Crêpes (Crêpe Cake)

Ingredients

- 20 thin crêpes (use your favorite batter recipe)
- 2 cups pastry cream or whipped mascarpone filling
- Berries or chocolate shavings for garnish

Instructions

1. Layer crêpes with a thin spread of filling in between each.
2. Chill for 2 hours before slicing.
3. Garnish with berries or dust with cocoa.

Filet Mignon au Jus

Ingredients

- 2 filet mignon steaks
- Salt and pepper to taste
- 2 tbsp olive oil
- 1/2 cup beef stock
- 1/4 cup red wine
- 1 tsp Dijon mustard
- 2 tbsp butter

Instructions

1. Season steaks and sear in olive oil (3–4 minutes per side). Remove and rest.
2. Deglaze pan with wine and stock, stir in mustard.
3. Simmer, whisk in butter. Serve sauce over steaks.

Caramelized Onion and Goat Cheese Tart

Ingredients

- 1 puff pastry sheet
- 3 onions, caramelized
- 1/2 cup goat cheese
- 1 egg, beaten
- Thyme, salt, and pepper

Instructions

1. Preheat oven to 400°F (200°C).
2. Lay out pastry on a baking sheet, prick with fork.
3. Top with caramelized onions and goat cheese. Sprinkle with thyme.
4. Brush edges with egg and bake for 25–30 minutes until golden.

Chèvre with Honey and Walnuts

Ingredients

- 1 log goat cheese (chèvre)
- 2 tbsp honey
- 1/4 cup toasted walnuts
- Crackers or baguette

Instructions

1. Plate goat cheese. Drizzle with honey and sprinkle walnuts.
2. Serve with toasted baguette slices or crackers.

Tartare de Bœuf

Ingredients

- 1/2 lb high-quality beef tenderloin, finely diced
- 1 egg yolk
- 1 tbsp Dijon mustard
- 1 tbsp capers, chopped
- 1 tbsp shallots, minced
- 1 tbsp parsley
- Dash of Worcestershire
- Salt, pepper, and olive oil

Instructions

1. Combine all ingredients gently in a chilled bowl.
2. Shape into a round and serve immediately with toasted bread or fries.
3. Optional: Top with egg yolk for classic presentation.

Madeleines au Chocolat (Chocolate Madeleines)

Ingredients

- 1/2 cup unsalted butter (melted, plus extra for pan)
- 2/3 cup sugar
- 2 eggs
- 1/2 tsp vanilla extract
- 1/3 cup all-purpose flour
- 1/3 cup cocoa powder (Dutch-processed preferred)
- 1/2 tsp baking powder
- Pinch of salt

Instructions

1. Whisk eggs and sugar until pale and fluffy. Add vanilla.
2. Sift in flour, cocoa, baking powder, and salt. Fold in gently.
3. Stir in melted butter. Chill 1 hour.
4. Preheat oven to 375°F (190°C). Butter and flour madeleine pan.
5. Spoon batter into molds, bake 8–10 mins. Cool and optionally dip in melted chocolate.

Salmon en Papillote (Salmon in Parchment)
Ingredients

- 2 salmon fillets
- 1 small zucchini, julienned
- 1 carrot, julienned
- 4 lemon slices
- Fresh thyme sprigs
- Salt, pepper
- 2 tbsp olive oil or butter
- Parchment paper

Instructions

1. Preheat oven to 400°F (200°C).
2. Cut parchment into heart shapes. Place salmon in center, season.
3. Top with veggies, lemon, thyme, and a drizzle of olive oil.
4. Fold and crimp edges to seal.
5. Bake 15–18 mins. Open with flair at the table.

Pan-Seared Foie Gras with Balsamic Reduction

Ingredients

- 2 slices fresh foie gras
- Salt and pepper
- 1/4 cup balsamic vinegar
- 1 tsp honey

Instructions

1. Chill foie gras slices 10 minutes before searing.
2. Score and season. Sear in hot skillet (1–2 mins per side).
3. Reduce balsamic with honey until syrupy.
4. Plate foie gras, drizzle with reduction. Serve with brioche toast or poached pear slices.

Mousse au Chocolat (Classic Chocolate Mousse)

Ingredients

- 6 oz dark chocolate
- 3 eggs, separated
- 1/4 cup sugar
- 1 cup heavy cream
- Pinch of salt

Instructions

1. Melt chocolate, cool slightly.
2. Beat yolks with sugar until pale. Mix into chocolate.
3. Whip cream to soft peaks, fold into chocolate.
4. Whisk egg whites with salt until stiff, fold in.
5. Chill 4 hours. Serve with shaved chocolate or whipped cream.

French Pistachio Macarons
Shells:

- 1 cup almond flour
- 3/4 cup powdered sugar
- 2 large egg whites (aged)
- 1/4 cup granulated sugar
- Green gel food coloring

Filling:

- 1/2 cup unsalted butter, softened
- 2 tbsp pistachio paste
- 1 cup powdered sugar

Instructions

1. Sift almond flour and powdered sugar.
2. Whip egg whites, adding sugar gradually until glossy peaks form.
3. Fold dry into meringue, add color.
4. Pipe onto parchment, rest 30–40 minutes.
5. Bake at 300°F (150°C) for 14–16 mins.
6. Sandwich with pistachio buttercream.

Canelés de Bordeaux

Ingredients

- 2 cups whole milk
- 2 tbsp butter
- 1 vanilla bean or 1 tsp vanilla extract
- 1 cup sugar
- 1 cup flour
- 2 egg yolks + 1 whole egg
- 1/4 cup dark rum

Instructions

1. Heat milk, butter, and vanilla. Cool.
2. Whisk eggs and sugar, add flour, then milk mixture slowly.
3. Add rum. Chill 24–48 hours.
4. Preheat oven to 450°F (230°C), butter canelé molds.
5. Bake 10 mins at 450°F, then 45 mins at 350°F (175°C) until dark and caramelized.

Pâtisserie du Jour (Pastry of the Day)

Rotate daily with:

- Éclairs with flavored cream
- Mille-feuille with vanilla custard

- Paris-Brest with praline cream

- Lemon tartlets with toasted meringue

- Raspberry financier with basil-infused glaze

Create a blackboard or printed card describing the day's selection, fresh from your kitchen.

Pistachio Frangipane Tart

Ingredients

- Tart shell (pâte sucrée or store-bought)

- 1/2 cup unsalted butter

- 1/2 cup sugar

- 1 egg

- 1/2 cup ground pistachios

- 1 tbsp flour

- Optional: apricot jam, raspberries, or poached pear

Instructions

1. Preheat oven to 350°F (175°C).

2. Cream butter and sugar, add egg, then pistachios and flour.

3. Spread frangipane in tart shell.

4. Top with sliced fruit or jam.

5. Bake 30–35 mins until golden. Cool and dust with powdered sugar.

www.ingramcontent.com/pod-product-compliance
Lightning Source LLC
LaVergne TN
LVHW061950070526
838199LV00060B/4055